The Inflatable Crown
Balloon Hat Book

Sinop, Turkey

Somewhere in Mongolia

Turkana District, Kenya

Table of Contents

How to Speak Balloon Hat

The Inflatable Crown
Balloon Hat Book

Addi Somekh and Charlie Eckert

A Melcher Media Book

chronicle books · san francisco

The relationship between people and hats is ancient and powerful. Throughout history, wherever you find human beings you'll find an interest in some form of headdress. "Dressing the head" is satisfying to the wearer, and it also makes a statement to everyone else. People feel crowned—separated and enlarged.

—*Mary Holmes,*
art historian

Addi Somekh, a.k.a., the Certified Balloonatic, at work in Lodwar, Kenya

eras and film, a couple of sleeping bags, just one change of clothes, and, as our parents said, "a crazy idea."

For three years we lived on the road, sleeping in cheap motels, on overnight trains, and in more bus stations than I could even count. We never had too much of a plan—just show up in a new town and try to make balloon hats for people in their natural, everyday environments. Whether it was a flower vendor in Saint Petersburg, schoolchildren in Vietnam's Mekong Delta, goatherds in the Sahel Desert of West Africa, a truck driver out in the scrub of East Texas, or a family of refugees in Bosnia, the reaction was the same. At first, confusion. Then intrigue. And finally, exhilaration. The balloon hat had the ability to bridge language and cultural divides and, for a few moments, remind us of how much we all have in common.

Four years, 100,000 balloons, and 10,000 pictures later, I can happily say we do live on a planet where laughter and happiness is spoken by all, a planet where the balloon hat is warmly welcomed and worn in any home—be it castle, tract house, or mud hut.

—Charlie Eckert,
balloon hat photographer

Photographer Charlie Eckert in Fort Thompson, South Dakota

be great if we could go around the world, make balloon hats for people and photograph them?"—the idea being that every human is born with the ability to laugh and have fun. By introducing balloon hat fun to random places around the world (and documenting people's reactions with photographs), we could offer evidence that we, the people of the planet Earth, at this moment, are more alike than we are different.

In no time, it seemed we were on our way—six incredible journeys through Central America, Europe, Africa, Asia, the Balkans, the Middle East, and the United States with nothing more than one backpack full of balloons, another filled with cam-

Seven Reasons to Twist Balloons

MeKong Delta, Vietnam

The gift of a balloon hat is a great way to make someone's day. Here are some common situations where twisting balloons has been known to work wonders.

Showing Gratitude. If you want to show people appreciation for something they've done—or just for being who they are—try a balloon flower or hat. Seeing you put the time and energy into a unique, handmade gift right before their eyes shows people that you care.

Celebrating Birthdays. Throughout history, a person honored in a public ceremony is often given a special headdress. Making a balloon hat for the birthday boy or girl is a modern way to continue this ancient tradition. Plus, it makes for great photo album pictures.

Making Friends on the Road. When visiting another city or country, balloon hats are a very easy, direct gift to those you meet along the way. By offering something interesting and novel, and by inspiring some laughter, you can help create a level of familiarity that might otherwise take weeks to foster.

Cheering Up a Sick Friend. Balloon flowers definitely light up a sick room, with both happy colors and good vibrations. Equally important, the process of watching a hat being made is more novelty and action than many sick people see all week.

Procrastinating. Whenever you feel the urge to drop what you are doing and avoid it for as long as possible, practicing your balloon-twisting skills is a much more productive escape than TV, video games, solitaire, or staring at the wall. Not only do you avoid stress, you develop a useful talent at the same time.

Earning Money. Instead of the same old job, try this. The enterprising twister can work for tips in restaurants, parks, fairs, busy street corners, or even for an hourly wage at parties. Plus you'll meet tons of new people.

Being the Life of the Party. Next time you're at a picnic or party that seems like it's moving in slow motion, you can come to the rescue. Balloon headdresses instantly loosen up the crowd and pump energy into the party. People will thank you for it!

Keep on Twistin'

International Balloon

The Crowning Touch

International Balloon

Introduction

Queens, New York

Before you proceed any further, a word of caution: The contents of this book will definitely pump you up. You will learn a new form of communication, a language without words that speaks to all. What you will learn may become something you do for friends at parties or a lifelong affair, but it will certainly teach you a new way of engaging people. I'm talking about balloon hats.

I first glimpsed the magic of balloon hats on a Halloween in New York City. Nobody among our friends had costumes, but a guy named Addi (a.k.a., the Certified Balloonatic) was carrying the makings of an incredible experience. Opening a mysterious denim pouch, he revealed a rainbow of latex—more balloons than I had ever seen in one place. A few twists here, a chain of ballies there, a couple of dingies, and finally a curly on top, and three minutes later and three feet taller, I was officially crowned. We couldn't walk more than a block without being stopped. People clapped and cheered. I had lived in New York my whole life, and never before had I seen this sort of reaction from complete strangers.

By the next morning, the question had to be asked: "Wouldn't it

How to Use This Book

Cairo, Egypt

The Inflatable Crown teaches you how to make balloon hats with simple, clear, step-by-step instructions. The book comes with a pump and 30 Qualatex® balloons. These balloons will last through the first section of the book, at which point you'll want to buy your own balloons.

So that you can see exactly what each hat is supposed to look like, every set of instructions begins with a full-page photograph, taken on our world travels, of somebody wearing the hat, and ends with a smaller picture of the hat alone. It might help to refer to the completed hat in case you ever get confused while making it.

We've rated each hat as either beginning, intermediate, or advanced (though everything is easy enough to learn with an hour or two of practice); and these groups correspond roughly to *The Inflatable Crown*'s three sections.

The first part of the book teaches you "How to Speak Balloon Hat." You'll learn fundamental skills, including how to inflate, twist, and hold balloons. Then come three simple but effective hats. Anybody who works through this first section should be able to star at a birthday party.

If you want to "Keep on Twistin", next come six high-quality hats and an ornament called the dingie. By practicing these hats, you'll learn more skills, develop an eye for detail, and gain a better understanding of what balloons can and can't do.

"The Crowning Touch" is the final third of the book, where we explore more fantastic hats and showstopping skills like the curly and weaving. Once you know the fundamentals and some fancy ornaments, advanced hat-making is about coming up with your own combinations and designs. The book culminates with a look at how to let your imagination run wild through the fun, funky art of improvisation.

If you want to see more pictures and read more stories about balloon twisting after you finish the book, check out our website at www.balloonhat.com. And if you have any further questions about how to make hats, go to our Frequently Asked Questions (FAQ) section at www.inflatablecrown.com.

A last word before you begin: You might notice that the word "p*p" appears in the book. We spell it with an asterisk (*) instead of an "o" because if you say the word too much it might happen.

Maha Sarakham, Thailand

11

SKILL 1
PUMPING

When making a balloon hat, you can't use just any old balloon. You need special balloons. These are officially known as 260s and often are referred to as twisting balloons. Unofficially, you might call them "those long skinny ones."

The first thing you will probably want to do with a twisting balloon is grab it, put it to your lips, and blow. Unfortunately, inflating 260s by mouth is a little tricky and takes some time to figure out. Fortunately, this skill is not necessary.

If you want to learn how to blow up balloons, we offer advice on page 96. For now, let's use a pump.

1

Start with the pump and 1 balloon.

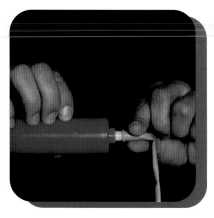

2A

Slide the lip of the balloon onto the nozzle of the pump and hold it in place with your fingers.

3c

2B

3A

Begin pumping.

3B

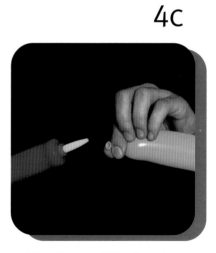

It takes about 20 seconds to fully inflate a balloon.

4A

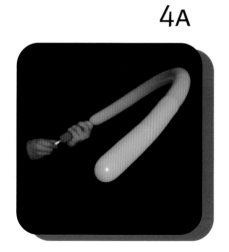

Pinch the neck of the inflated balloon...

4B

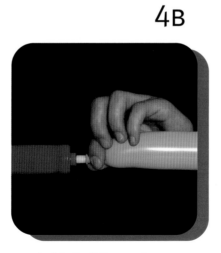

and slide it off the nozzle.

4C

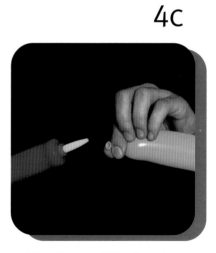

Voila! Next we will tie the balloon.

SKILL 2
TYING

Different people tie knots differently—go with what works best for you. Here is one way to tie the balloon.

IMPORTANT: Before tying the knot, get in the habit of letting a little bit of air out of the balloon. This makes it a little looser and more flexible.

1

Hold the balloon between your index finger and thumb. Let a little air out if the neck needs some slack.

2

Use the thumb and first two fingers of your other hand to pinch the balloon a second time just below your other fingers.

4A

Separate the two fingers to create a little space...

4B

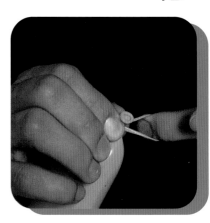

and tuck the lip of the balloon through the circle.

3A

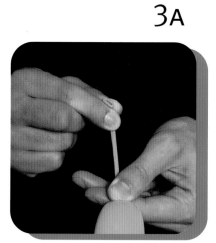

With your first hand, stretch the neck of the balloon...

3B

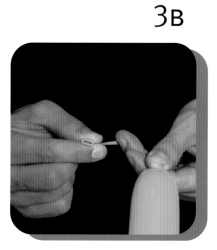

and wrap it around the two fingers of your other hand...

3C

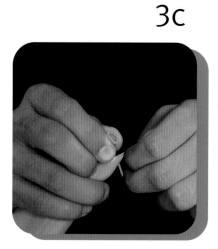

forming a full circle.

5A

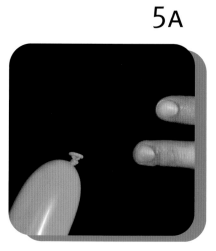

Slip your fingers out of the circle...

5B

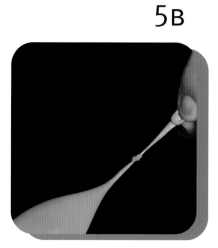

and tighten the knot (optional).

5C

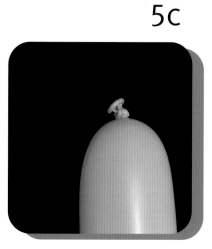

Put this balloon aside. You can use it in a moment for the **long loop**.

SKILL 3
HOLDING & TWISTING

When twisting a balloon, there are two important things to remember. First, hold the balloon with one hand and twist with the other. Second, always twist the balloon in the same direction: toward your body.

1

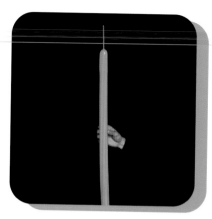

Inflate the balloon, leaving four inches uninflated. We call this uninflated part the "tail." The tail is important because the air needs extra space to fill when you make twists.

2A

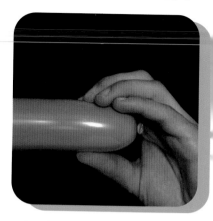

Gently squeeze the balloon at the point where you want a twist.

3

Twist the balloon with your other hand. Give it three full turns toward your body.

2B

4

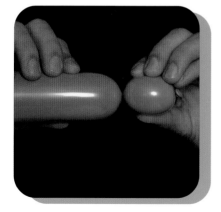

A round, roughly 1-inch shape like this is called a "ballie." The part that's twisted is called the "joint."

5

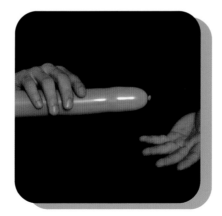

Now let go with your twisting hand. Notice that the twist you've made instantly unravels. Next up: locking.

SKILL 4
THE SELF-INVOLVED LOCK

Locking balloons turns them into something much more than plain old latex. Suddenly you can make neat shapes. Here you make a simple lock by twisting a balloon around itself.

With the same balloon, make another **ballie**, just as before.

Hold the ballie at the joint so it doesn't unravel, and curl the balloon into an oval roughly the size of a person's head.

3

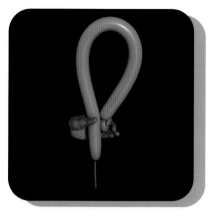

Continuing to hold the ballie at the joint, bring it against the other side of the balloon at the spot you've chosen.

4

Twist the large oval three times around.

5

This is the **self-involved lock**.

But before we go further, we must learn the all-important **security lock**.

SKILL 5
THE SECURITY LOCK

Every time you make a self-involved lock you must add a security lock. The security lock keeps your twists from coming undone and limits the damage to a hat if one section p*ps or springs a leak.

1

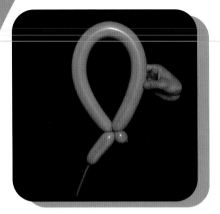

Note that the twist you just put in the **self-involved lock** was made in one direction only.

2

Now push the **ballie** into the loop and all the way around the existing joint. Once should be enough, but twice is always better. This is the **security lock**.

4A

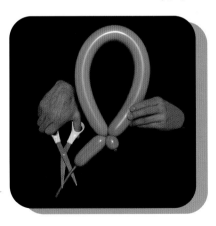

But if you snip the tail of the balloon with scissors after you've made a security lock, that section will be the only one that deflates.

3

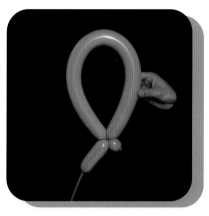

If you return the ballie to its original position, you can see that there is no change from the way the balloon looked before you added the security lock.

4B

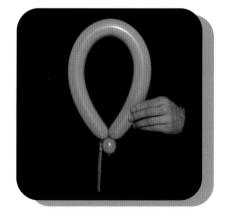

5

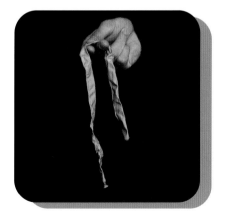

Without a security lock, your balloon would have ended up looking like this.

On the pages ahead, whenever we say "security lock" or "lock it," you should add a second direction to whatever twist you've just made.

SKILL 6
TEDDY BEAR TWIST

Now let's learn another type of twist and lock. The teddy bear twist creates a seal between sections of a balloon. It also changes the direction of the balloon by 90 degrees.

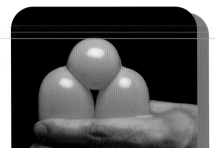

1

Inflate 1 balloon, leaving a 5-inch tail. Make two twists so that a **ballie** separates one large section of balloon from a 3-inch handle section. Remember to always twist in the same direction.

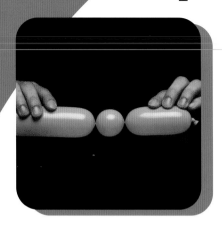

2

Bring the first and third sections together and hold them in one hand.

3A

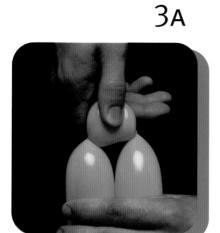

Pinch the ballie with your thumb and forefinger, pull it upward, and twist it three times.

3B

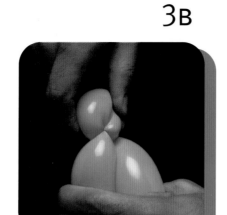

Don't be afraid to apply pressure. The balloons are surprisingly tough.

3C

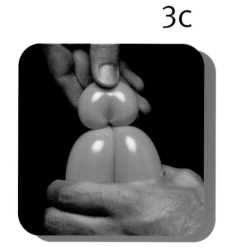

4

The **teddy bear twist** is a strong and effective lock. It keeps its shape when you let go.

5

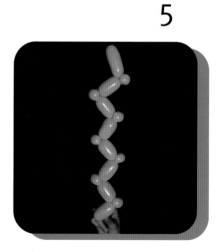

As an exercise, make as many teddy bear twists as you can.

Simple and graceful, the long loop has a lot of potential for future balloon hat action.

1

Fully inflate 1 balloon.

2

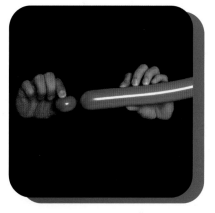

Twist a **ballie** at the end of the balloon.

3

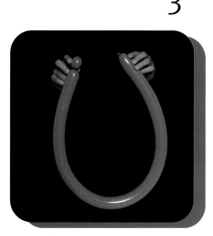

Bring the two ends of the balloon together.

4

Wrap the knot of the balloon twice around the joint of the ballie.

5

Add the **security lock**: Push the ballie into the loop and back around once or twice.

6

This is the **long loop**. Hold on to it; we'll use it soon on the **Martian Helmet**.

The swirly is an easy-to-make, visually impressive balloon trick. Not only do swirlies fit in many hats, but they also make great staffs for parades and marches.

1

Start with 2 fully inflated balloons.

2

Hold the knotted ends of the balloons together.

4B

3A

With your other hand, pinch 2 **ballies** and twist them together.

3B

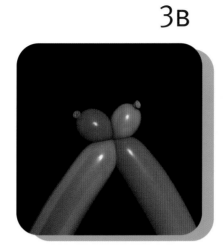

The balloons will look like this.

4A

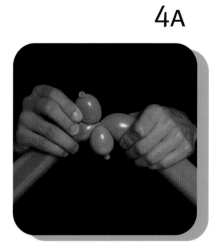

Add a **security lock**.

5A

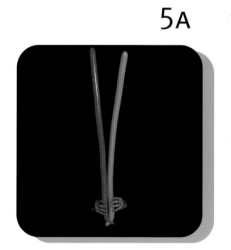

Begin to swirl, firmly but slowly.

5B

5C

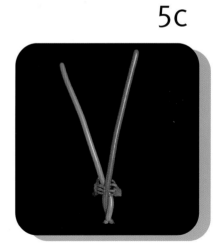

5D

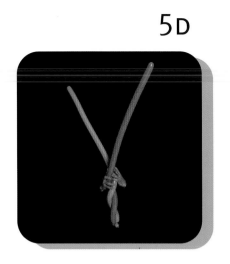

5E

5F

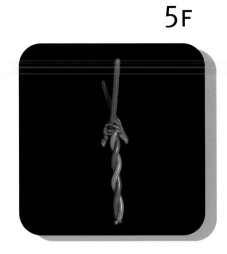

6B

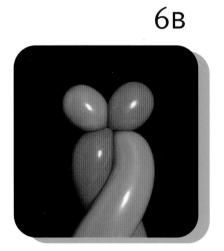

7A

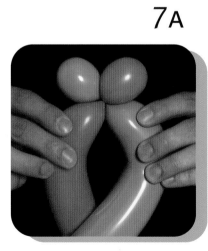

Make a security lock by slightly separating the swirly and tucking one of the ballies through.

7B

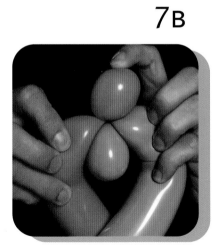

5G

5H

6A

As you reach the end of the **swirly,** pinch 2 ballies with one hand and twist them together.

8

You have just made a swirly! Soon we'll use one for the **Unicorn Hat.**

SKILL 9
BALLIES

A string of ballies is always a crowd pleaser, and it makes any hat look better—both more regal and more spirited. Practicing ballies is also a great way to develop finger coordination.

1

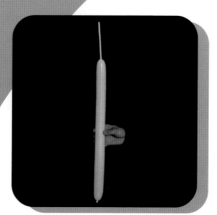

Inflate 1 balloon with a 6-inch tail.

2A

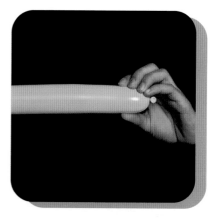

Make a **ballie** at the knotted end of the balloon.

2B

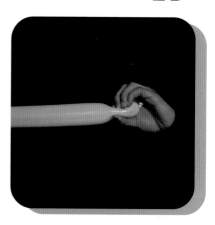

As you know, pinching the balloon marks the spot where you want to twist.

2C

Remember that one hand holds while the other twists. Give each ballie three full turns toward your body.

2D

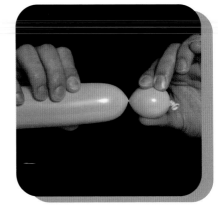

3A

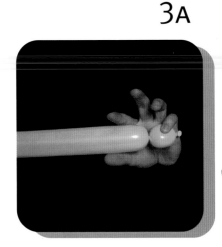

To make a string of ballies, you must hold on to the first ballie. If you let go, it will unravel. Hold the first ballie between your pinkie and palm.

5B

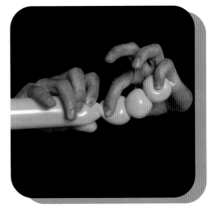

You need only to hold the first ballie and the opposite end of the balloon to keep the string from unraveling.

6

Twist in as many ballies as you have room for.

7A

Remember to always twist the ballies in the same direction.

3B

Free your index finger and thumb to pinch and twist again. (If this is difficult, try holding the first ballie bet-ween your knees—or have a friend hold it for you.)

4

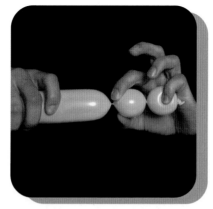

Repeat the twisting motion with your twisting hand, turning the balloon in the same direction as before.

5A

Now move on to the third ballie, while keeping a grip on the first.

7B

7C

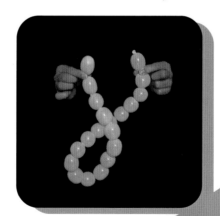

7D

Make a **self-involved lock** between the first and last ballies to keep the string from unraveling.

7E

Notice how much longer the string of ballies is compared to the original size of the balloon. When the balloon is twisted, the air fills the tail and the balloon expands.

7F

SKILL 10
BASIC BASES

1. INSTANT CLASSIC BASE

The first step in creating a balloon hat is to make a base. The base is the foundation. You make it first, and everything else builds up from there.

We're going to start with three simple bases, each one made from a single balloon.

When making a base, always remember to first make sure it will fit the head of the person who'll wear the hat. You want a balloon hat to be comfortable—not too tight and not too loose. If you don't measure the head first, you can spend a lot of time on a hat and then find out that it doesn't fit.

The instant classic base is simply a self-involved lock fitted to a person's head and completed with a security lock.

Previous Page
Sa Pa, Vietnam

1

Grab a volunteer and fully inflate 1 balloon.

2

Twist a **ballie** at the knotted end of the balloon.

6A

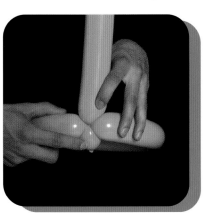

Add a **security lock** by twisting the ballie into the circle and around the joint.

3

Holding the ballie in one hand and the rest of the balloon in the other, wrap the balloon around the back of the wearer's head.

4

Note the spot where the ballie meets the other end of the balloon.

5

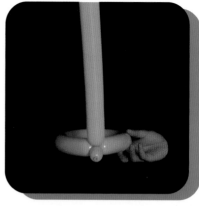

Now twist the ballie around the balloon to complete the headband.

6B

You have now made the **instant classic base**.

2. UNIT SHELL BASE

The unit shell base involves a simple adaptation to the instant classic, yet looks very different.

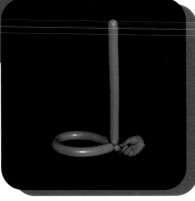

Make the **instant classic** base again.

Now twist a **ballie** at the end of the pole.

Stable and sturdy, here is the **unit shell base.**

3

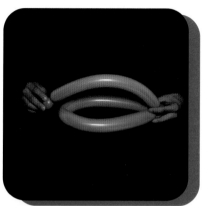

Pull the ballie down toward the opposite side of the h eadband.

4

Wrap the ballie into the headband.

5

Add a **security lock** by wrapping the ballie around the joint in the other direction.

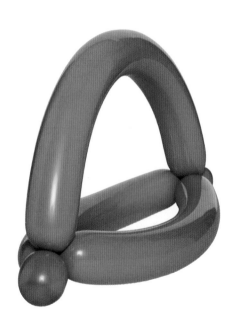

3. FANCY V BASE

How can something be so simple, yet look so fancy?

1

Fully inflate 1 balloon.

Hold the balloon at both ends and place the middle of the balloon at the back of the wearer's head.

6A

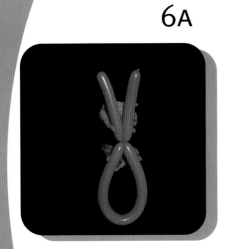

Grab and twist the loop with your other hand.

6B

Two full turns will do it.

7A

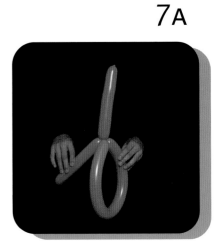

Now add a **security lock**.

3

Bring the ends together and hold them with one hand.

4

With your other hand, pinch the two sides together at the person's forehead and then let go with your top hand.

5

Now lift the balloon off the person's head, maintaining the size of the circle.

7B

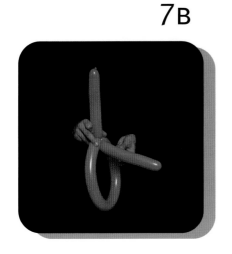

7C

Behold the **fancy V base**. Now you know three bases.

Unicorn Hat

BEGINNER

3 BALLOONS NEEDED

Now that we know the three basic bases, we will use them in making three hats that are specially designed to incorporate your new skills and look supercool.

Simply by connecting an instant classic base and a swirly, you can experience the totem power of the Unicorn Hat.

1

Begin with 1 **instant classic base** and 1 **swirly**.

2

Pinch the base's headband at the point opposite the pole.

3A

Connect the knotted ends of the swirly to the headband at that point...

3B

by tucking the headband between the **ballies**...

3C

and twisting the ballies twice on the outside of the band.

4

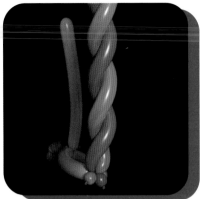

Add a **security lock** by wrapping another ballie around the base.

5A

Now take the pole of the base...

5B

and push it through the swirly about 1/3 of the way up from the bottom.

5C

6

When you don the **Unicorn Hat**...

your balloon adventure begins!

Martian
Helmet

BEGINNER

3 BALLOONS NEEDED

Warning: The Martian Helmet is a psychic superconductor. Proceed with caution.

1

Start with 1 **unit shell base** and 2 **long loops**. (Use three different colors.)

2

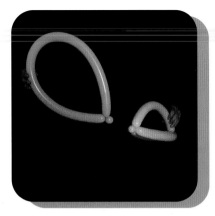

Bring the **ballie** of one long loop together with one of the ballies on the base.

6

Tuck the middle of the long loop into the joint of the ballie.

3

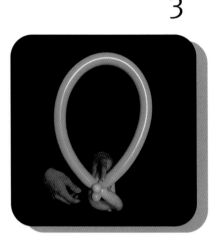

Twist those ballies together.

4

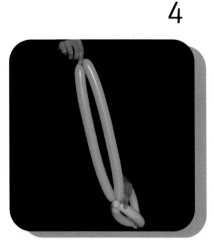

Find the middle of the long loop and pinch it.

5

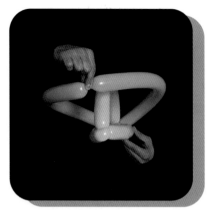

Bring the long loop down toward the ballie at the opposite side of the base.

7A

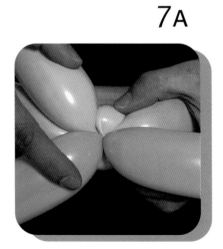

Lock it by wrapping the ballie once around the long loop.

7B

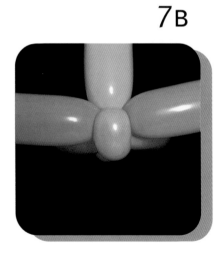

8

Take the second long loop and twist its ballie around the first two ballies. Lock it by twisting the three ballies together.

9

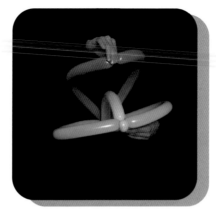

Find the middle of the second long loop and give it a pinch.

10

Bring the second long loop toward the ballie on the other side of the base.

11A

Twist the ballie into the second loop.

12A

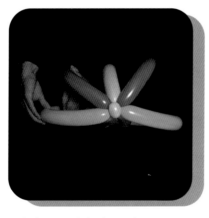

Grab one of the lower bars, plus the one above it.

12B

Bring the upper one down through the inside of the hat.

12C

11B

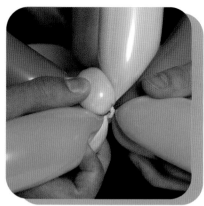

11C

The final step accents the colors and adds a **security lock**.

Now put on your hat and feel the Martian energy!

Ballie Brain Protector

BEGINNER

3 BALLOONS NEEDED

Now you get to incorporate your ballie-making skills into a hat that's as safe as it is hip.

1

Start with 2 **fancy V bases** and 1 balloon with a 6-inch tail.

2A

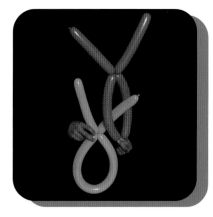

Pinch the middle of the headband of one base and twist that into the joint of the other base.

2B

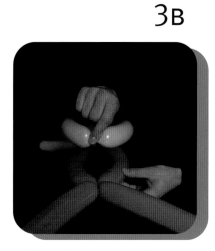

3A

Pinch the middle of the second headband.

3B

Bring it down between the limbs of the first base (one limb goes through the loop), and twist together.

4A

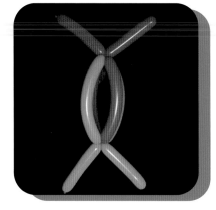

Lock it by rotating one limb around the joint. As you can see, the V bases form a helmet with four limbs sticking out.

4B

Pull one of the bars inside the one next to it (as we did with the **Martian Helmet**). This serves as a **security lock**.

5

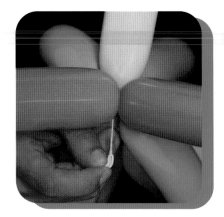

Wrap the tie of the third balloon around one of the joints.

9

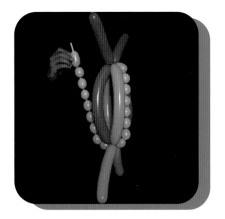

Make another set of 7 or 8 ballies, beginning at the joint. Remember to hold on to the first ballie.

10

Twist the joint of the last ballie into the opposite joint on the helmet.

11

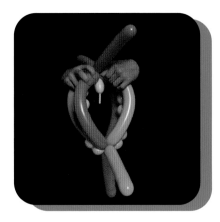

Add another security lock.

6

Make 7 or 8 **ballies**, beginning at the joint.

7

Twist the joint of the last ballie around the opposite joint on the helmet.

8

Add a security lock.

12A

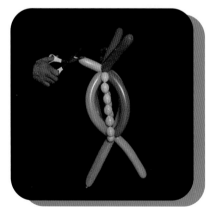

Cut off the surplus balloon. Snip the tail to avoid a loud p*p.

12B

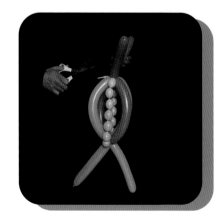

Here is the Ballie Brain Protector. It may look like one simple hat, but by adding more balloons, you can turn it into dozens of different hats. Learn how to do this later in the "Improvisation" section.

International Balloon Photo Gallery No. 1

Tokyo, Japan

Rajasthan, India

Manhattan, New York

Somewhere in Mongolia

El Faiyûm, Egypt

Los Angeles, California

Maha Sarakham, Thailand

Royal Center, Indiana

Sarajevo, Bosnia

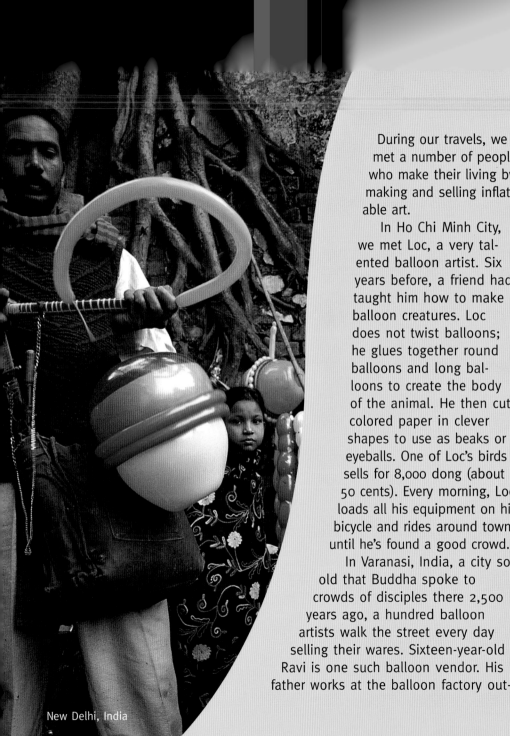

New Delhi, India

During our travels, we met a number of people who make their living by making and selling inflatable art.

In Ho Chi Minh City, we met Loc, a very talented balloon artist. Six years before, a friend had taught him how to make balloon creatures. Loc does not twist balloons; he glues together round balloons and long balloons to create the body of the animal. He then cuts colored paper in clever shapes to use as beaks or eyeballs. One of Loc's birds sells for 8,000 dong (about 50 cents). Every morning, Loc loads all his equipment on his bicycle and rides around town until he's found a good crowd.

In Varanasi, India, a city so old that Buddha spoke to crowds of disciples there 2,500 years ago, a hundred balloon artists walk the street every day selling their wares. Sixteen-year-old Ravi is one such balloon vendor. His father works at the balloon factory out- side of town and brings home balloons for his five kids to sculpt and sell on the streets. Ravi works seven days a week.

Ravi also makes a fascinating balloon horn made of a long balloon, cut on both ends, and two pieces of bamboo. Each balloon end is pulled tightly around an inch or so of bamboo, then tied down with string. When a person blows into a bamboo end, the balloon inflates and pushes air through the horn. Each horn takes about five minutes

Ho Chi Minh City, Vietnam

Antigua, Guatemala

Bangkok, Thailand

Varanasi, India

to make and sells for 2 rupees. By the end of the day, Ravi usually has made 50 rupees (about $1.50).

Other interesting styles of balloon art we found included funny balloon puppets in Antigua, Guatemala. Using large and small round balloons, 260s, glue, and cutout paper shapes, the artists created two-foot-tall faces. In Belgrade, Yugoslavia, we found a man sitting on the side of the road selling balloon puppets of a style found throughout Europe. They're made of balloons filled with fine sand that can be molded into different shapes. Yarn is used for hair and two small stickers for eyes. Finally, on the streets of Bangkok, Thailand, we found maybe the most fascinating and inventive balloon idea of all.

After inflating a latex glove and tying off the bottom, the Thai balloon artist paints fingernails and a design on the glove's palm, attaches it to a stick, and adds a nest of round balloons at the wrist.

Each of these styles of balloon sculpting developed independently, continents apart. Each has its own materials and techniques, and its own sense of beauty. Only the job description remains the same: Make something colorful and fun enough, and you'll be sure to draw crowds and make new friends.

63

Field Goal Fever

INTERMEDIATE

3 BALLOONS NEEDED

Sometimes you need to decorate the head of a guest of honor. Here's a hat designed to be both quick AND slick.

1

Begin with 2 **instant classics** and 1 **swirly**.

2

Pinch the middle of one of the instant classics.

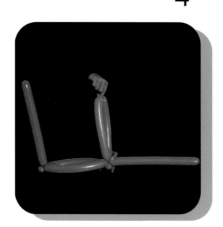

3

Take the **ballie** of the other instant classic and twist it in at the spot you're pinching.

Tokyo, Japan

4

Now pinch the middle of the headband of the second instant classic.

5

Pull the pinched spot down toward the other ballie and twist the ballie around the middle of the headband.

65

6

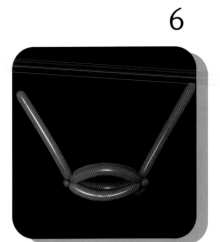

Pull one of the upper bars of the crown inside the one below it.

7

Decide where you want the poles to poke through the swirly.

8

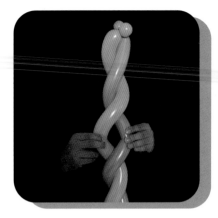

Pull open a space for each pole.

9A

Push the first pole through.

9B

Repeat on other side.

Let the games begin!

SKILL 11
DINGIES

1. DRY DINGIE

Also referred to as a boinger, doinker, or dinglybopper, the dingie is an ornamental piece that is very effective in exciting a crowd and adding flair and movement to your hats.

We'll show you two methods of making a dingie, and then a way to detach a dingie from the rest of its balloon.

1

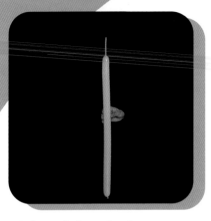

Inflate 1 balloon, leaving a 3-inch tail.

2

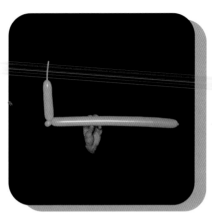

Make a **teddy bear twist** about 5 or 6 inches from where the tail begins.

6A

Now squeeze the ballie in a *downward* motion. If you are holding the tail the right way, you will be able to push the air through it till it reaches the top.

3

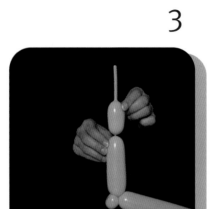

Twist a 1½-inch **ballie** right below where the tail begins.

4

With your fingers, cover all of the tail except the very tip.

5

With your other hand, cover the ballie you just made.

6B

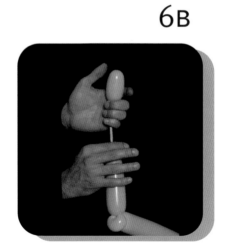

7

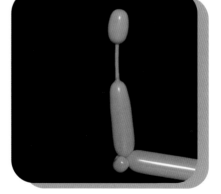

Let go—you have just created a quality **dingie**.

Next: The **wet dingie**.

2. WET DINGIE

The wet dingie is created by sucking the air through the balloon instead of pushing the air with your fingers.

1

Follow Steps 1 to 3 on pages 68–9 so that your balloon looks like this.

2A

Now push down on the balloon while you suck the air upward with your mouth.

2B

See? The **wet dingie** is more efficient and entertaining.

2C

And just because it's called the "wet" dingie doesn't mean it comes with slobber on it! It can be done so quickly and smoothly that people barely notice the balloon has been in your mouth.

3. DETACHABLE DINGIE

A dingie can be freed from the balloon it's attached to, so you can use it as an ornament anywhere you want. And the operation can be done quickly and quietly so long as you've secured your teddy bear twist well—give it two or three extra twists.

1

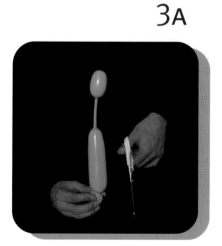

Twist a new joint 1 inch away from the **teddy bear twist**.

2

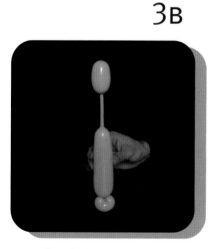

With scissors, cut the balloon at the joint.

3A

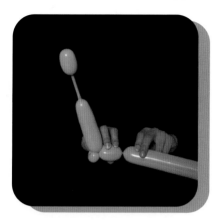

Unless the balloon is extremely full and tight, the cut should be effortless and p*pless.

3B

The **detachable dingie** can be added to any hat at any time.

Oval Pierce

The classiest of all balloon hats, the Oval Pierce is fit for a museum but made for your head.

1

Begin with 1 **instant classic base**, 1 **long loop**, and 1 balloon with a 6-inch tail.

2

Pinch the middle of the headband and connect the **ballie** from the long loop into it. Add a **security lock** by wrapping the ballie around the joint in the other direction.

3

Pinch the middle of the long loop. Make a ballie on the top of the instant classic and twist it into the middle of the long loop.

4

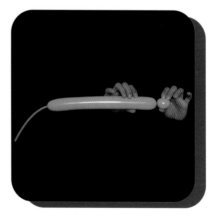

Twist a ballie at the knotted end of the balloon with the 6-inch tail.

El Faiyûm, Egypt

5

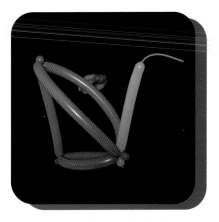

Twist that ballie into the ballie of the long loop at the front of the headband. Add a security lock.

6

Making sure to hold the base in a fixed position, twist 6 or 7 ballies.

7

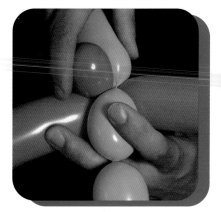

Twist the end of the string of ballies into the ballie of the instant classic base. Make a security lock.

8

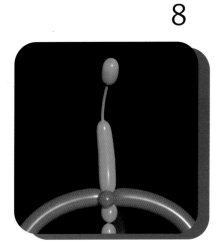

Do the **dingie**. Adjust to perfection.

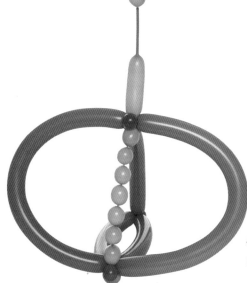

An instant collector's item!

Space Invader

INTERMEDIATE

4 BALLOONS NEEDED

Not all balloon hats are from the planet Earth.

1

Begin with 1 **unit shell base**, 2 fully inflated balloons, and 1 balloon with a 4-inch tail.

2

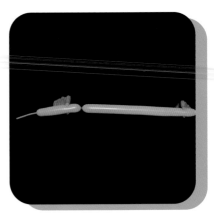

Make a twist about 3/4 of the way up the balloon with the 4-inch tail.

5

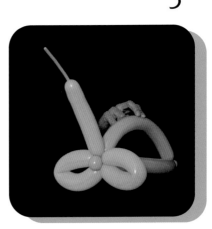

Twist the center around the **ballie** of the unit shell.

3

Wrap the tie of the balloon around this joint, creating a circle.

4A

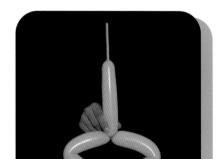

Pinch the bottom of this circle and bring it upward...

4B

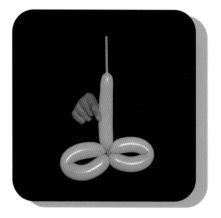

then twist it into the first joint.

6A

Take the long balloons and, with their knots pointed toward the back of the hat, insert them through the little loops.

6B

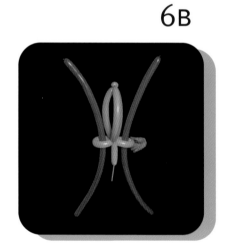

7

Pinch the knotted ends of both balloons and twist 2 ballies together.

8A

8B

Attach these 2 ballies to the ballie at the back of the unit shell base.

8C

9

Pull the long balloons so they're tight. Put the hat on someone's head, then separate the long balloons outward.

Stand back!

The Space Invader needs a lot of space.

Head Hunter

What good is a balloon hat without a head? Just ask the Head Hunter.

1

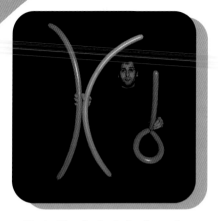

Start with 1 **instant classic**, and 2 fully inflated balloons.

2

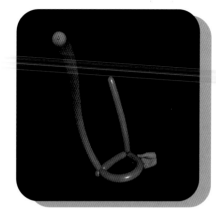

Make a **ballie** at the end of an inflated balloon, and twist it into the side of the instant classic headband. **Security lock**.

4C

5A

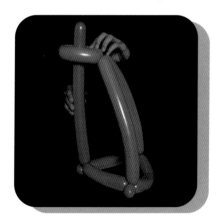

Insert the pole of the instant classic through the "bagel" and push the bagel about halfway down the pole.

3

Twist the other end of the same balloon into the opposite side of the headband. Security lock again.

4A

Now grab the top of this arching balloon and make a **self-involved lock** the size of a large bagel. Twist it around a few times. (Don't worry about a security lock.)

4B

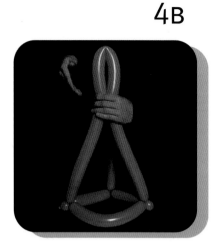

5B

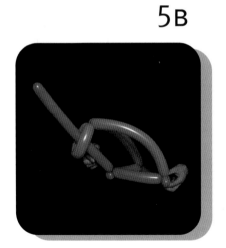

6

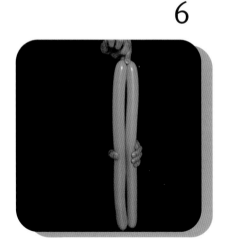

Now take the other fully inflated balloon and twist it in the middle.

7

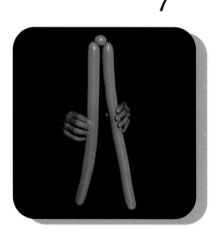

At this spot, make a ballie.

8

Teddy bear twist the ballie.

9

Twist this balloon's teddy bear twist into the joint of the bagel.

(Spear not included.)

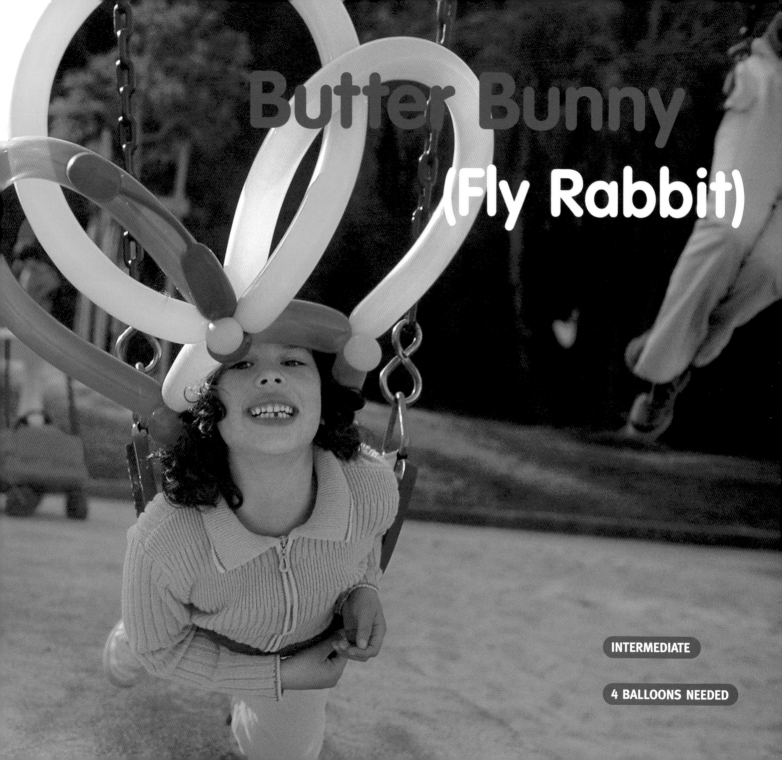

Butter Bunny
(Fly Rabbit)

INTERMEDIATE

4 BALLOONS NEEDED

So far, all the hats we've shown you are built using single-balloon bases. There are countless ways to build a base using two or more balloons. Two new bases are used in this hat and the next, just to give you an idea of what's possible. The Butter Bunny (Fly Rabbit) involves a pretzel-like base.

The Balloonatic's personal favorite, the Butter Bunny (Fly Rabbit) is a hat so fine it deserves two names.

1

Start with 3 fully inflated balloons and 1 balloon with a 5-inch tail.

2

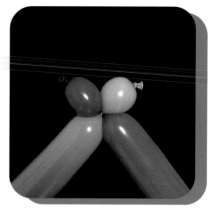

Twist 2 **ballies** together at the knotted ends of two fully inflated balloons.

6

Slide the third fully inflated balloon through the two loops of the pretzel.

Previous Page
San Francisco, California

7

Bring the ends of this fully inflated balloon together and make a **long loop** so that it's locked inside the hat.

8

Twist the ballie of the long loop into the front of the base. (Make sure that the bottom half of the long loop stays in front of the pretzel shape of the base).

3

Wrap the joined balloons around a person's head to find the point where the balloons should meet. Pinch the balloons at that point and twist them together. Add a **security lock**.

4

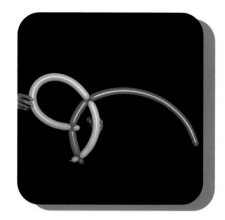

Twist the end of one of the balloons into the base on the same side.

5

Twist the other balloon into the opposite side of the base.

9

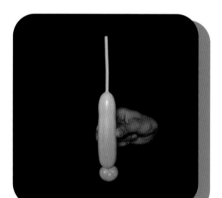

Make a **detachable dingie** from the balloon with the 5-inch tail.

10

Twist the detachable dingie's **teddy bear twist** into the ballie of the long loop at the front of the hat.

Cleared for takeoff.

Latex
Falcon

INTERMEDIATE

4 BALLOONS NEEDED

Here's another way to build a base with two balloons. With a wingspan of 4 feet and a funky factor of 10, the Latex Falcon is flying fast into the fashion future.

1

Begin with 3 fully inflated balloons and 1 balloon with a 4-inch tail.

2A

Make the same shape you made using Steps 2 to 4 in the **Space Invader** (pages 76–7).

2B

2C

Twist 2 ballies together at the *unknotted* ends of the 2 fully inflated balloons.

3

Thread 1 long balloon through each of the loops.

San Francisco, California

4A

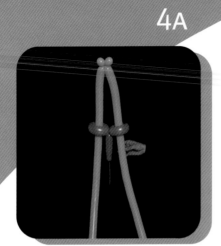

Pull the balloons through until the triangle at the top is small enough for a wearer's head.

4B

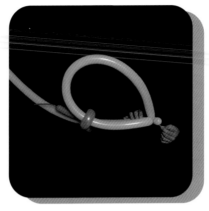

Pull the knotted end of one of these balloons back toward its ballie.

5

Then use the knot to make a **long loop**.

7C

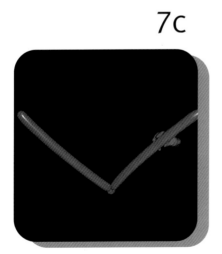

8

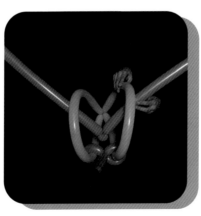

Pull this shape through the long loops.

9

Twist the **teddy bear twist** into the joint at the front of the hat. Use the tail at the top of the hat to make a **dingie**.

6

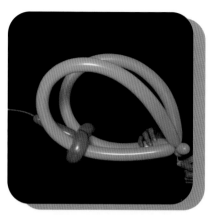

Do the same with the other balloon.

7A

Make this shape with the third fully inflated balloon, just as we did in Steps 6 to 8 of the **Head Hunter** (page 81–2).

7B

As you can see, there are many ways to make a base. If you use your imagination, it's hard to find a head that a hat won't fit.

Queens, New York

International Balloon
Photo Gallery No. 2

Tromsø, Norway

Harlem, New York

Calcutta, India

South Beach, Florida

Brooklyn, New York

Helsinki, Finland

Tamale, Ghana

East Los Angeles, California

Blow It Up

You've probably tried to blow up a 260 and realized it's not as easy as it seems. That's because the tube shape of the 260 and its narrow opening make its resistance much greater than that of a regular round balloon. The trick is to turn your lips and tongue into a pressure valve, similar to the act of whistling. This most efficiently forces air into the balloon. Blowing up balloons with your mouth offers speed, showmanship, and makes certain techniques possible, the curly (which comes next) being the most important of them. However, blowing them up also requires more energy and can result in dizziness or, in extreme cases, health problems. People with throat or sinus problems should probably stay with the pump.

If you want to go for it, there are a few things to keep in mind. Just as if you were learning to play the trumpet, it takes some time to figure out how to hold one's lips and blow. Rest the balloon on the inside of your lips. Then pinch the balloon about two inches up the neck. You want to begin by inflating this small section, then fill up the rest of the balloon.

You don't want to feel pressure or pain inside or beneath your ears. If this happens, you will not inflate the balloon, and you may even hurt yourself. Instead, focus on bringing air from your diaphragm directly to your lips. Keep in mind that there is more than one way to do this. Different people have come up with different techniques. Try the following trick to get the feeling of how the air should come out.

With the pump, fully inflate a balloon, then let all the air out, which will stretch out the balloon considerably. Then try blowing it up with your mouth. It should be less difficult, and will let you feel how best to hold your lips and tongue.

And finally, don't get frustrated. It took Addi a month of steady practice to finally get it. As with learning to ride a bike, it seems impossible before you learn to do it, but with practice, all of a sudden it clicks.

Shenyang, China

MeKong Delta, Vietnam

Rajasthan, India

SKILL 12
CURLY

The curly is one of the great feats of balloon twisting. Not only does a curly make any hat look fancier and wilder, but the act of making one marvels any audience.

The critical part of the trick is to inflate the balloon while it's wrapped around your fingers. The difficult part is to inflate the balloon with lung power. But we'll first teach you how to make a curly with a pump.

Whether you do the puffing or a pump does, the first six steps of the curly are the same.

1

First you must stretch out a balloon. Fully inflate the balloon, but don't tie it.

2

Slowly let out the air.

3

Notice how much longer the balloon has become compared with its original size.

4

Hold out the first two fingers of one hand.

5

Place the sealed end of the balloon at the base of your fingers, holding it in place with your thumb.

6A

Begin wrapping the balloon evenly and firmly, but not too tightly.

6B

Make sure it doesn't get tangled as you wrap it on.

7A

An assistant is necessary when you make a **curly** using a pump.

6C

6D

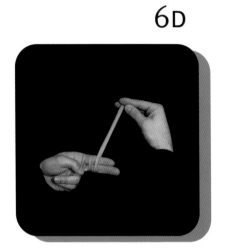

6E

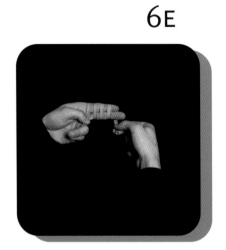

It helps to have long fingers.

7B

Once the balloon is wrapped around your fingers...

7C

the assistant can then use the pump...

7D

to make the curly spring to life.

8A

Or, if you like to blow up balloons by yourself, start after Step 6E with the balloon wrapped around your fingers.

8B

Begin to blow air into it...

8C

and witness a latex marvel.

8D

This is not easy. It takes a lot of practice.

8E

9

But balloons don't get much loopier than this.

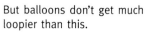

Master Blaster

ADVANCED

4 BALLOONS NEEDED

For the Thunder God in us all, the Master Blaster is all about power and magnitude.

1

Begin with 1 **instant classic base**, 1 **long loop**, 1 fully inflated balloon, and 1 **curly**.

2

Twist the **ballie** of the long loop into the center of the headband, opposite the pole.

6

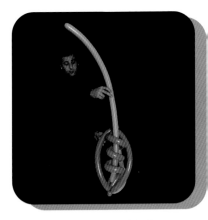

Slide the fully inflated balloon through the curly, with the tie at the bottom of the hat.

3

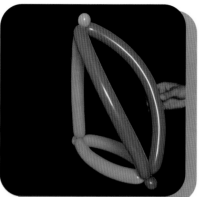

Twist the center of the long loop into the top of the pole.

4

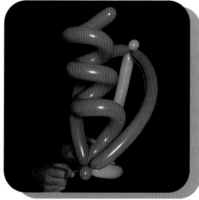

Wrap the knot of the curly around the ballie at the base of the long loop.

5

Form a ballie on the other end of the curly and connect to the ballie at the top of the hat.

7

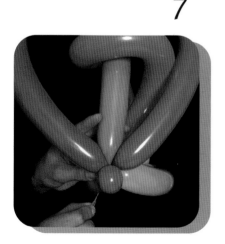

Wrap the tie around the ballie of the headband.

Put on the Master Blaster and rule your own little world.

Good Old Round Balloons

Jaipur, India

When your fingers need a rest, try spreading the joy with the classic round balloon. This is especially true when visiting other communities and countries. They are easy to pack, easy to blow up, and make a quick and colorful gift without the time and energy needed to make hats. They double as snazzy, festive decorations. But the best reason to give out round balloons is the simplest: watching your new friends blow them up and quickly invent new games for their new toys.

Belgrade, Yugoslavia

Tamale, Ghana

Varanasi, India

Rajasthan, India

MeKong Delta, Vietnam

Ilijaš, Bosnia

Princess Crown

ADVANCED

3 BALLOONS NEEDED

A pretty face deserves a quality crown—the Princess Crown is sweet, stunning, and always in fashion.

1

Begin with 1 **fancy V base**, 1 **curly** and 1 fully inflated balloon.

2

Twist one end of the curly into an end of the fancy V base.

3

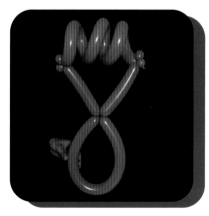

Twist the opposite end of the curly into the other end of the fancy V base.

San Francisco, California

4

Slide the fully inflated balloon through the curly.

5

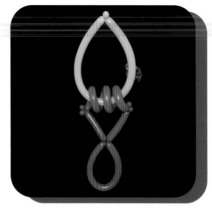

With both ends of the fully inflated balloon, turn it into a **long loop**.

6

Attach the ballie of the long loop into the joint of the fancy V base.

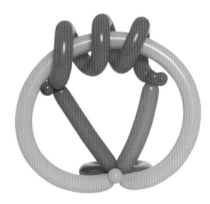

All hail the Princess Crown!

Dysfunctionally Large Hat

ADVANCED

4 BALLOONS NEEDED

When someone asks for the biggest hat you can make, make it so large it's Dysfunctionally Large.

1

Begin with 1 **instant classic base**, 2 fully inflated balloons, and 1 **curly**.

2

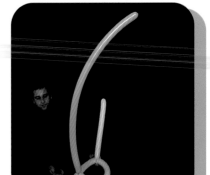

Make a **ballie** on the knotted end of one fully inflated balloon and twist it into the side of the headband.

6

Twist one end of the curly into the top of one long balloon.

3

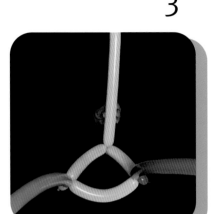

Do the same on the opposite side with the other long balloon.

4

About 7 inches up from the bottom, twist the 2 long balloons.

5

Make a ballie at the top of the instant classic's pole and twist it into the joint where the long balloons meet. Add a **security lock**.

7

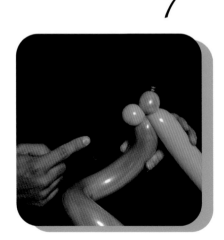

Twist the opposite end of the curly into the top of the other long balloon.

Hey.
You asked for big.

Polar Bear Lounger

ADVANCED

5 BALLOONS NEEDED

In addition to offering comfort and prestige, the Polar Bear Lounger shows an appreciation for the good things in life.

1

Start with 1 **unit shell base**, 1 fully inflated balloon, 1 balloon with a 5-inch tail, and 2 **curlies** (optional).

2

Twist the middle of the fully inflated balloon.

3

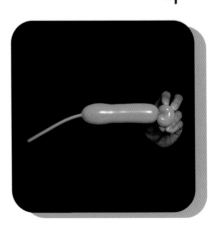

Twist that joint into the **ballie** at the front of the base.

4

Make a **detachable dingie** out of the balloon with the 5-inch tail.

Coney Island, New York

Twist the dingie's **teddy bear twist** into the ballie on the front of the base.

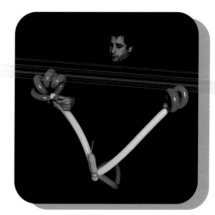

Make a **self-involved lock** with each of the curlies by forming a ballie at one end and wrapping the knot around the ballie's joint.

Attach the curlies to the limbs.

**Stand back.
This hat is not for
the meek of heart.**

SKILL 13
WEAVING

Weaving is a form of balloon twisting that transforms your hats from wacky to classy. By weaving together two strings of ballies, the result is a sleek and stylish headband. Because it takes more time to make, weaving is best used for special occasions.

1

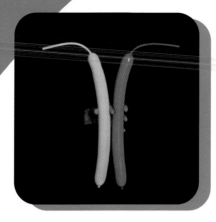

Begin with 2 balloons that have 6-inch tails.

2A

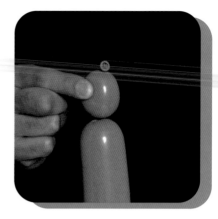

Make a **ballie** at the knotted end of each balloon.

3

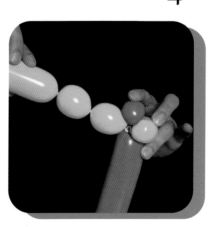

Twist the 2 ballies together, then give them a **security lock**.

Previous Page
Tokyo, Japan

4

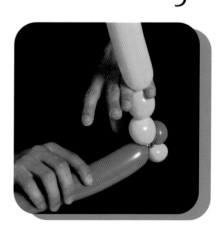

Twist 2 more ballies into one of the balloons.

5

Now we need to twist ballies into the second balloon without letting go of the first balloon's new ballies, so hang on to them with the fourth and fifth fingers of your holding hand.

2B

Optional: If you want to make the weave look especially nifty, you can tuck away the knots. Just take one of the knots...

2C

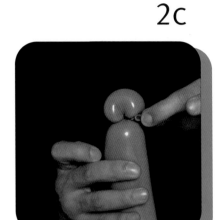

and wrap it around the joint of its ballie, making the joint look like a **teddy bear twist**.

2D

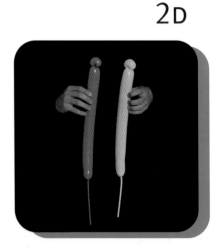

Do the same with the other balloon.

6

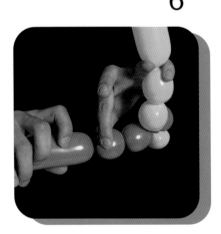

Now twist 2 more ballies into the second balloon. Make them the same size as the other ballies.

7

Bring the two strings of ballies side by side.

8

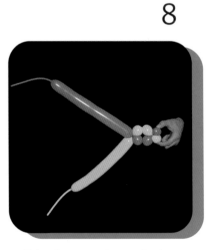

Twist them together at the last joints on each string.

9A

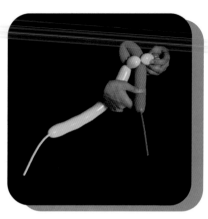

Security lock the weave by pushing the end of one of the balloons through the space between the 4 new ballies.

9B

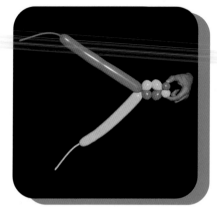

This is the first section of the pattern. Now let's do it again!

10

Make 2 more ballies on one of the balloons.

12B

Security lock them.

12C

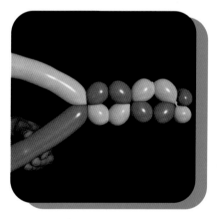

Now you have 2 sets and know the basic pattern.

13

Following the same steps as before, keep on twisting until you run out of room. Use a security lock on each set.

11A

Again, hold on to those 2 ballies as you put 2 ballies into the other balloon.

11B

12A

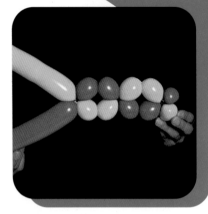

Twist the balloons together at the last joints on each string.

14A

When you are about to run out of room, make a single ballie on one of the balloons and use it to do a teddy bear twist.

14B

Make another teddy bear twist on the other balloon, then twist together the 2 teddy bear twists.

14C

Cut off the surplus.

14D

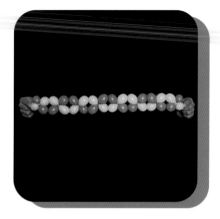

The weave should look like this.

15

To make a cool headband, just wrap the weave around somebody's head and twist the ends together. If the weave isn't long enough, connect the ends with a third balloon.

The Pro Efficient Solo Method

Here is another, quicker way to do the weaving technique.

Follow the regular weaving instructions up to Step 3, so that you have a V shape. With one of the balloons, make as many ballies as you can. While holding on to the joint between the 2 balloons, place the final ballie between your legs, which will keep it from unraveling as you begin to weave. Now, with the second balloon, make two ballies at a time. Interlock the two balloons after every set of two ballies, as in the regular weaving instructions. Don't forget the security lock. At first this might seem tricky, but with practice it's quick and easy.

Tiara

ADVANCED

2 BALLOONS NEEDED

Elegant enough for a black tie ball or a backyard tea party, the balloon Tiara proves you can be dignified and playful at the same time. Created by a slight change in the weaving pattern, the Tiara makes every day a special occasion.

1

Follow Steps 1 to 3 of the weaving instructions (pages 118–9).

2

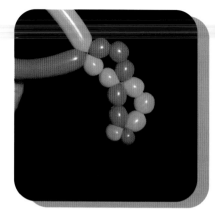

However, instead of making a 2 x 2 pattern, make a 2 x 3 pattern.

3

To finish, follow Steps 14 to 15 in the weaving instructions (pages 121–2). To ensure the **Tiara** stays on comfortably, connect an uninflated balloon to both ends to make a headband.

Flower

INTERMEDIATE

3 BALLOONS NEEDED

Just as a bouquet of flowers never fails to brighten your spirit, a balloon flower made and delivered with love sends a clear message—it's a homemade way to show affection and appreciation.

Also, for those times when a person doesn't want to wear a hat (due to vague fears about messy hair, looking goofy, or a repeat of some traumatic childhood p*pping experience), a balloon flower is a great substitute.

1

Part One: The Petals
Inflate 3 balloons leaving 3-inch tails. Use 3 different colors.

2

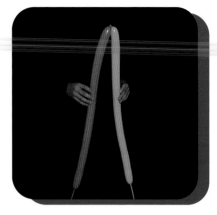

Tie the knots of 2 of the balloons together.

6A

Security lock that twist, too.

3

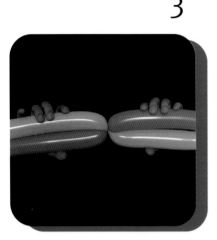

Twist the 2 balloons together about 9 inches from their knots.

4

Weave one limb through, forming a **security lock**.

5

Move another 9 inches down the balloon and make a second twist.

6B

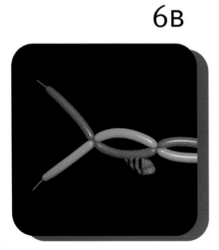

Now you have a pair of 9-inch loops.

7

To make the third set, bring the loose ends of the 2 balloons down to the first joint.

8

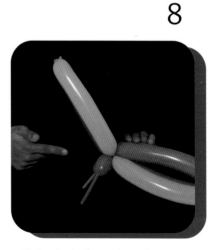

Twist the balloons into that first joint.

9A

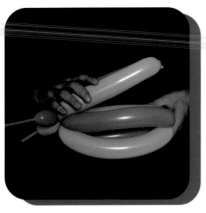

Bring all 3 sets of loops together in alternating colors...

9B

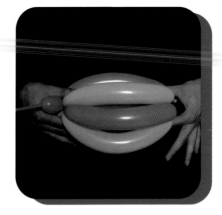

and hold the group with a hand on each side, as if it were a hamburger.

10

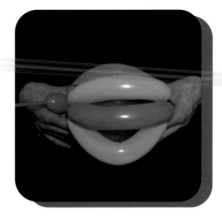

Push the edges of the "hamburger" together from both sides so that the edges meet in the middle. Don't worry, the balloons won't p*p.

12B

13

Your hamburger now has 6 petals.

14A

Cut off the 2 pieces of surplus...

11A

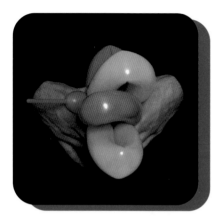

When each hand can touch the other side...

11B

reach across and grab the far side of the burger.

12A

With your other hand, grab the top 3 loops, pull them upward, and twist them around in a complete circle.

14B

and the flower petals will look like this.

15

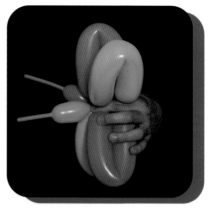

Part Two: The Stem
Twist a joint about 3 inches below the tail of the third balloon.

16

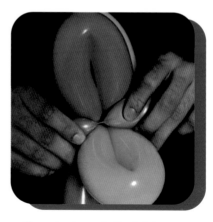

Then simply push the joint between two petals. It will stay lodged there.

You can make a stem with either a straight balloon...

or a curly.

A surprise bouquet can make your sweet's knees weak.

Glamorous
Ring

INTERMEDIATE

2 BALLOONS NEEDED

For that special someone who deserves a (somewhat) lasting symbol of your devotion, we offer you...the Glamorous (balloon) Ring.

1

Start with 1 balloon containing 1 inch of air and 1 balloon containing 4 inches of air.

2

Using the **dingie**-making principle, make a **ballie** at the end of the balloon with 1 inch of air.

5B

3

Twist the balloon right underneath the ballie and hold it there.

4

Tie a knot at the bottom of the ballie. This might be tricky at first, but you'll get the hang of it quickly.

5A

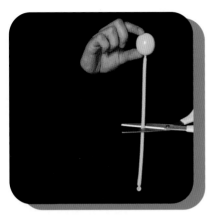

Cut off the surplus 6 inches below the ballie.

6A

Tie another knot to form a small uninflated loop. This is where the person's finger will fit.

6B

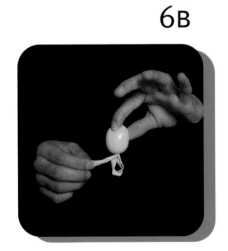

7

After forming the finger loop, cut off the surplus again.

8

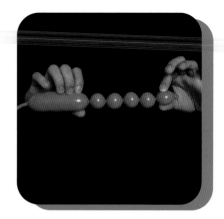

Now take the other balloon and twist 5 small ½-inch ballies at the knotted end.

9

Tie the knot into the joint of the last ballie to form a 5-ballie circle. It's best to double-tie this one.

10A

Cut off the surplus, first by cutting the balloon to deflate it...

11B

12A

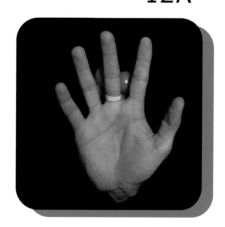

Place your finger through the loop and get ready to dazzle.

10B

and then again to trim the remainder.

11A

Place the finger loop into the 5-ballie circle.

12B

Balloon Bodysuits: The Next Frontier

Manhattan, New York

The balloon bodysuit is the logical extension of the balloon hat—instead of decorating only the head, you decorate the entire body. A suit can range from the subtle and functional to the massive and outrageous. Even at a costume party, balloonwear stands out because of the colors, the size, and each garment's one-o'-a-kind nature.

There are no rules to making the bodysuit. The best way to learn is by trial and error, but a good place to start is by wrapping balloons around a person's waist, wrists, and ankles. These serve as connection points, and you can then attach balloons from one point to another, creating a kind of web.

For extra wackiness, try attaching some helium balloons.

Busua, Ghana

Manhattan, New York

Copenhagen, Denmark

Mendocino, California

improvisation

Jaipur, India

Now you know how to twist balloons. What next?

You may want to invent some hats of your own. It can be as simple as adding different ornaments to one of the hats we've already made. Or you can start from scratch and let your imagination go wild. If you keep twisting long enough, you will develop your own repertoire of bases, shapes, and ornaments. For advanced twisters, one of the best ways to discover new shapes and new hats is to improvise.

Improvisation is fun because it makes you feel connected to the moment and surroundings at hand. Plus, the people you're twisting for know they are seeing a tailor-made creation—which makes the hat not just a hat, but an *event*.

If the idea of being spontaneous and going out on a limb in front of people makes you nervous, don't be, because here's how to do it.

What Is Improvisation?
Improvisation is the act of making things up on the spot—whether it's a musical solo, a comedy performance... or a balloon hat. When improvising, you can't go back and change or fix the work. Out it comes; once it's done, it's done, and it won't come out the same the next time. That's what makes the skill so beautiful and special.

When inventing, we begin with an idea or feeling but proceed without knowing exactly where it will lead. It's like being an explorer in uncharted territory. For this reason there is always a sense of excitement in seeing what improvisation will produce.

Just because spur-of-the-moment creation happens without a set plan doesn't mean that it's aimless. Successful improvisation depends on practice. As with everything else in life, whether you're playing the violin or dribbling a basketball, the more you practice, the better you get. Think of practice as collecting an arsenal of fireworks, and the act of improvising as detonating the fireworks: The more practice you have, the bigger and fancier the bursts of light.

We often improvise without realizing it. When we talk to someone, we almost always create our ideas and sentences as we speak. When we ride a bike, we judge and adjust to the road and stay ready to react. In fact, any job that involves on-the-job training—even working behind an ice-cream counter—involves making up things as you learn.

Improvisation is one of the most useful talents that human beings possess. It allows us to create things we did not know we were capable of. We all have the gift but can still work to develop and strengthen it. Improvisation is mysterious and necessary—and, best of all, constantly surprising.

How to Improvise with Balloons
Chances are that you have been creating from the very beginning of this book. Blowing up three or four balloons, then twisting and connecting them at random is a spontaneous experiment.

In devising your own hats, think of the balloons as building blocks. Once you have a number of blocks (**ballies**, **swirlies**, **dingies**, etc.), all you have to do is arrange them in a way that is physically stable and pleasing to the eye. So that the hat will hold up, *remember to begin with the base*, and build from there. As for what shapes work, that's where your personal taste comes in—it's whatever you think is right.

Here are some exercises that can help you to think in a spontaneous way.

VARIATIONS ON A THEME

Pick a hat from earlier in the book and make three regular versions of it. Now add to or decorate each hat in a different way, using dingies, swirlies, or your own creations. This exercise is designed to help you get past the natural tendency to go with what's familiar. It can also help you invent new ornaments. In this case, we start with a Ballie Brain Protector.

To succeed, planning alone is insufficient. You must also be able to improvise.
—*Isaac Asimov, author*

EXPERIMENT WITH A SHAPE

Pick one shape, any shape (here we use a long loop that's twisted in half), and make three hats that are considerably different but all incorporate the shape somewhere in the hat. This exercise helps you see that one shape need not be used the same way all the time.

You must be able to do things that are, quite simply, beyond your abilities. When you succeed, the abilities themselves move forward.

—*David Rothenberg, author*

INCORPORATE YOUR SURROUNDINGS

This exercise is great improvisational practice. It encourages you to really open up to your environment. For starters, try using balloons that replicate or play off the colors a person is wearing in his or her hat. Then try to incorporate unique shapes taken from the setting you're in—for instance, make bull horns when you're twisting at the rodeo. As you gain confidence in your ability to mimic odd shapes, take requests from your audience.

Expect the unexpected and play with a sense of urgency.
—*Sun Ra, cosmic band leader*

Wichita, Kansas

Inverness, Scotland

Kokrobite, Ghana

JUST GO CRAZY

Play around at random and see what comes out. Each time you do this, you learn something new: what works, what doesn't work, mistakes to avoid in the future, and shapes to remember. Even huge corporations do this—they just call it research and development.

Imagination is more important
  than knowledge.
              —*Albert Einstein, scientist*

Two final points to keep in mind. First, don't be afraid of mistakes. Whenever we try something new, something is bound not to work the first time (a balloon might even p*p!). Making mistakes is an important way to learn. If we are too afraid of making mistakes, we limit our capacity to grow.

And finally, remember that the most important thing is to have fun. Take risks, but don't let them stress you out. Find your own pace that's challenging but fun. Now you're on the road to inventing your own individual balloon hat style!

Queens, New York

International Balloon Photo Gallery No. 3

Sofara, Mali

San Antonio, Texas

Maha Sarakham, Thailand

Trujillo, Honduras

Somewhere in Mongolia

Jaipur, India

Saint Petersburg, Russia

London, England

Shenyang, China

Milwaukee, Wisconsin

Acknowledgments

From the moment this project was conceived, we instantly began to ask for favors and help from friends and strangers. Here are some of the people who fed us, gave us places to sleep, and offered help, advice, and encouragement.

Guatemala: Todos Santos Cuchumatán Proyecto Lingüístico Español/Mam, Juan Ramirez. **Nicaragua**: Mr. "Lingo" Alvin Hing, Corn Islands Peace Corp Crew. **England**: Pipa Galea, Emeka Onono. **Scotland**: Mary Smith and Gowanbank Barn. **Ireland**: Mairead and Sean DeLaney and family, Wessy Kassa. **Northern Ireland**: Peter Worth. **France**: Kevin O'Brien. **Germany**: Thomas Grigat. **Denmark**: Mille Mapjeka. **Holland**: Voucha and Kalai Herrick, Homegrown Fantasies Coffee Shop. **Norway**: Knut Hohle, Ingvald Guttorm, Karajok Barneskole. **Finland**: Iina Olinki and Riku Puustilli. **Russia**: Sergie Nikitan in Moscow, Tatiana Kobalenko and Kira Levina in St. Petersburg. **Poland**: Wiesiq Kozub, the mysterious English girl with the luscious lips. **Prague**: Katka Zapletalova. **Ghana**: Henry NeiBoy Oudo,

The Balloonatic's mom sewing his balloon apron (reenactment).

the Royal Princess Crown Hotel Crew, Andy, Big Andy, Little Andy. **Burkina Faso**: Bruno, Jean Luc, Antoine Bambara, Bationo "Vincent" Manore. **Mali**: Nuofoo, who only got us stranded in the desert once. **Kenya**: The Great Dr. Donald S. Gilchrist, Dr. Tony Barrett, John Ebenyo Kawalathe. **Japan**: Ono San, Akasaka San, Sato San, Rika Kanda, Hirokazu Sugiyama and family, Kenji Kowamoto. **Vietnam**: Phil Dolan and Hiên Nguyen, Luc the Driver, Wendy Madrigal, Josh and Nancy Gnass. **China**: Ming Chi Bao, Tom Kirkwood and Cowboy Candy (big, big "thank you"), Jeff Keidel, Shahin Kianpour and Kirsha

The can-do man in Mongolia, and King of the Press Conference, our good friend Bold.

Kaechele (thanks for providing sanity), the always impressive Anna Shields, Travis Hicks, Ewrin Zaat, Louis Jenseny. **Mongolia**: Bold, Gotoff, Odbileg and Gerelma, Ch. Nyamdorj, Roger Gruys, Didi Kalika and the Lotus Children's Center, Perenlei Sendzoo, Dorjpalam, Junji Masuda. **Thailand**: the people who drove us around and introduced us to everyone in Maha Sarakham, Weerachon Puttpradit. **India**: Ian Winn, Barry and Lars, Mr. John Majors. **Hungary**: Monika Muranyi. **Bosnia**: Sean Moffatt and everyone at USAID, Nadja Karahmet. **Serbia**: Dragon Radonovich, Natashaha and Jelena, Ana, Zoran, Nikoli, Zorana, Ivana, Studio B, Bora (for the plum wine). **Turkey**: Hale Ozen in Sinop, Nilgün Eke in Istanbul. **Israel**: Yuda, Drora and Aviram Gavish; Rachel Somekh; Chana Rubinovitch; Prof. Sass Somekh (essential help). **Palestinian Authority**: Hassan and Wali Asous, Pizza Inn. **Egypt**: Mohamed Waly, Yossi Amitai. **California**: Shell Saunders and family, everyone at The Feed, Tiarra Car Club, Alberto Michel, Joe Roma, Krissy Ramirez, Don and Ruby Brown, Bob and Roslind Thomas, our man in Venice Gerry Fialka, Nissan and Carmela Pardo, Ron Pardo, Brad Williston, Anh Vi Dao, Luis Estrada and Balloonabilities, Loyd Mooney and Around the World Books, Antoinette Maillard, Besedka Johnson, David Martin, Amacker Bullwinkle, Fred Burke, Fred Drake, Rev. Herb Schmitt, Dr. Paul and Charlene Lee, Don and Julia Harrison (extra-strength help), Hamid Ezzatyar, Harrod Blank, Katherine Beires, Kalman Kaufman, Matt Callahan, Bruce Cantz, Harold Goldstein and Carol Streeter, Jim Bierman, Oceanic Arts, Marie Mandoli. **Nevada**: Heidi, Phil, Martin, Felice, the Great Sean Rooney, Danielle Dickson. **New Mexico**: Nancy Evans of Shiprock, DVS, Castillo Brothers Barber Shop, Pueblo of Zia, Albuquerque International Balloon Fiesta, Balloonmiester Alan Rector, Gay Jensen James, Debbie Fowler. **Texas**: Mark Granoff, The Street of Lights on 37th St. in Austin, Keith Grays, Stanley Marsh, Amarillo Helium Facility, Warren Rowsell. **Colorado**: Brendan and Katie McGivney. **South Dakota**: Ronette Kirkie Walton, Joseph Shields, Oliver Sully. **Wyoming**: the Currachett family—Alnina, James, and Jamie. **Kansas**: the boys at Fire Station 13B in Wichita. **Nebraska**: Kevin Welsh and family, the Ludz Brothers

(Dwayne, Dwight, Gordon, and Jerry). **Indiana**: Ken and Phyllis Martin, Dana Williamson, Glen's Barbershop in Royal Center. **Illinois**: Martin Hallanger, Cabrini Green Youth & Family Services, Jimmy Fitzgerald. **Wisconsin**: Zav Leplae and the whole Pumpkin World Crew. **Michigan**: Prof. Arwulf Arwulf, Matt Camp, Ana Furioso. **New York**: Ashlyn, Sarah, Charlotte, Aidan Moran (and Gerry and Sean); Gennie and Manny; Yudi Soffer; Megan Shields; Bob and Judy Goldman; Penny Peters; Shirley and Matthew Gabriner; Jeff Tiecher; Pete and Jack at the Chrysler Building; Debra Goldman; Laura Hanifen; Werner and Helen; Josh Kroner and Tamara Hunter; the always-entertaining Brendan Burt; Iceberg Athletic Club; Joe Lazzaro; John Sineno; David Stanford; David Parker. **Florida**: Uncle Charlie Barbash and Aunt Ruth, Marty and Ann Robinson, Lisa and the Tallahassee YMCA. **Louisiana**: Ann Marie Coviello and the Box of Wine Krewe (Long Live Dr. Larry), Sean McNally and Jen Knox, Ray "Rowdy" Sibley, Clara Connell, Villa Feliciana Medical Complex, New Orleans Klezmer All-Stars.

Behind-the-scene players and invaluable help: Andy Wermouth, Nancy Dillon, Jason Brown, Noah Thomas, Jan and Jerry James, Kristie Faber, Earl Slavitt, and "Hey Now" Hank Kingsley.

On the business side of things, we'd like to thank: Everyone at Melcher Media for giving us a chance—Charles Melcher, Gillian Sowell, Duncan Bock, Andrea Hirsh, Molly Cooper, and

Veteran emergency surgeon and our hero, Dr. Donald Gilchrist of Kenya (via Scotland).

Vincent helped us navigate the local bureaucracy of Ougadougou, Burkina Faso.

Megan Worman; Chronicle Books; Pioneer Balloon Company and Dan Flynn; Leonard Phillips and Gladstone Media; Manhattan Color Lab; in San Francisco, the New Lab and Robyn Color; and our legal counsel at Morrison and Foerster—Jennifer Ortega and Ken Suddleson.

Thanks to all the balloon hat models for their beautiful faces and personalities: Paloma Perez, Dawn at Your Nails on Washington St., Cali Callardo, Julian Mendez, Erin Ashford, Khalida Peterson, Jasmine Edwards, Koree Cox, Gregory Haynes (and Carmen for organization), AliKatt, Sasha and Vincent Harrison, Mary Bustamante, Sara Grasteit, Calynn and Christina Melara, Carson and Darby Rosenberg, the very flexible Nancy Luna, City Ballet School in San Francisco and Maya Collins,

The generous Jan and Jerry James and their home-away-from-home crash-pad in Santa Cruz, California.

Amanda Peet, Samantha Mednick, Maura Tuohy, Elizabeth Treese, and John Wickett and the Museum of the Exotic.

To all the people who came over and tested the instructions and gave good advice: Dan Huertas, John Bebe, Meredith Preble, Pat in the Hat, Mike Rosenberg, Greg Apodoca, and especially the keen eye of Daniel Packard.

Charlie Eckert would like to thank the following people for their logistical and emotional support:

The spirit of Charles W. Eckert, Adrienne and Todd Eckert, Eta and Sass Somekh, "Sweet" Crissie Ferrara, "Mad" Matt Lewis, Jeff Day, the spirit of Herb "Busy B" Meier, Talli Somekh, Teddy Li, an EXTRA SPECIAL super light thanks to Curt and Stino and the Creative Closets crew, Jerry Vezzuso, Frank Espada, the Moran clan, the Lambrinos clan, Jeff Meyer, Nicole Lemieux,

Andy Wermouth, winner of the much-coveted "Antoine Award for Excellence" in balloon-hat internshipping.

Aunt Roberta and Uncle Allen, Sean "AirMan" Ryan, Mittens, Foo, Arthur, Godzilla, Y'all, Chulo, Bugsy, Thrasher, Mel Rosenthal, "Big" Tom Muchowski, Mimi Lobell, Scott Davis, Erik Matheu, Fred Muench and Jodi Levine, Brendan White, Brian White, Nicole Schorr and Melanie McGillick, Mira Jensen, the McGivney clan, Will Schmidt, Jay Brown, Terrell Wick, Noah Thomas, Josh Chaffin, the worms that occupied my belly, Ana Morris, Eileen, Melissa Goldman, Grounds Keeper Willie, and the people of the planet Earth.

—Charlie Eckert

Charlie with Ana and Natasa as we are about to leave Belgrade, Yugoslavia.

The balloon twister would like to thank all these great people:

My nuclear family—Eta, Sass and Talli—for love and support, Pearl and Tim O'Brien, The Penny University for an education, Mary Holmes for hours of conversation and insight, Master C. K. Chu and T'ai Chi Chuan of New York, Jim Borrelli, Galen Rosenberg, all my peoples at KFJC 89.7 FM at Foothill College for setting me on the right course, Sex Mob for heavy doses of inspiration (Cassandra Wilson, Dave Alvin and Mudhoney all rule. So does Big Lazy.), big hug for Kristen Lee, Jeff Wilson, the Eckert family, the reference librarians at McHenry Library at UCSC for helping with all the needle-in-a-haystack questions, Bill Tracey, and the great city of Santa Cruz, California. Ultimate Thank You's to Tracy Hunter, whose beauty, depth, and crazy energy fueled my ability to make things out of balloons, and to Page Smith, whose memory continues to fill me with warmth, peace of mind, and gratitude. Thanks for checking out our book.

—Addi Somekh, Certified Balloonatic

If we forgot to mention you, we apologize in advance and promise to buy you lunch.

Send us pictures of your balloon hats! PO Box 3091, Los Altos, California 94024 or www.inflatablecrown.com.

151

This book was produced by Melcher Media, Inc.,
55 Vandam Street, New York, New York, 10013,
under the editorial direction of Charles Melcher.

Charles Melcher, Publisher
Duncan Bock, Senior Editor
Gillian Sowell, Editorial Manager
Andrea Hirsh, Director of Production
Megan Worman, Publisher's Assistant/Office Manager
Molly Cooper, Editorial Assistant

Special thanks to Carol Bobolts, Colin Dickerman,
Sara Gillingham, Chris Mitchell, Amy Novesky,
Victoria Rock, Gabriella Rotaru, Nathan Savage,
and Deb Schuler.

Printed in China.
Printing by C&C Offset.

ISBN 0-8118-2994-4

Distributed in Canada by Raincoast Books
9050 Shaughnessy Street, Vancouver,
British Columbia V6P 6E5

10 9 8 7 6 5 4 3 2 1

Chronicle Books LLC
85 Second Street, San Francisco, California 94105

www.chroniclebooks.com/Kids

Addi Somekh used Qualatex® balloons in all his
balloon hats. From the severe heat of Africa to the
freezing cold of Mongolia, Qualatex balloons always
rose to the occasion and performed incredibly well.
They are the easiest brand of balloons to inflate by
mouth and withstand the most twisting without
p*pping. Qualatex balloons come in a rainbow of
colors, and are made of 100% natural latex so
they're fully biodegradable.

The people at Qualatex also make a great pump. It
is compact, sturdy, and can inflate a whole 260 in
just seconds. Check it out!

Information on where to purchase Qualatex balloons
and several high-quality pumps is available by
calling 1-877-615-5376 or 1-316-685-2266 and
through www.Qualatex.com/TheInflatableCrown.

⚠ WARNING

CHOKING HAZARD Children under 8 years can choke or suffocate
on uninflated or broken balloons. Adult supervision required. Keep
uninflated balloons from children. Discard broken balloons at once.

The balloons provided in this kit are latex and should not be used by
anyone with a latex allergy.

The publisher, authors, and producer specifically disclaim liablility for
any loss or injury incurred as a consequence of the use and application,
either directly or indirectly, of any advice, information, balloons, or
pump presented herein.